WHITE WOLVES

YEAR

4

Stories from Different Cultures

KARINA LAW

Teachers' Resource for Guided Reading

A & C Black • London

Contents

White Wolves Series Consultant: Sue Ellis, Centre for Literacy in Primary Education

Reprinted 2010
First published 2007 by
A & C Black Publishers Ltd
36 Soho Square, London, W1D 3QY
www.acblack.com

Text copyright © 2007 Karina Law
Illustrations copyright © 2007 Matilda Harrison, Rosamund Fowler and Mike Phillips

The right of Karina Law to be identified as author and the rights of Matilda Harrison, Rosamund Fowler and Mike Phillips to be identified as the illustrators of this work have been asserted by them in accordance with the Copyrights, Designs and Patents Act 1988.

ISBN 978-0-7136-8510-7

A CIP catalogue for this book is available from the British Library.

This book is produced using paper that is made from wood grown in managed, sustainable forests. It is natural, renewable and recyclable. The logging and manufacturing processes conform to the environmental regulations of the country of origin.

Printed in Great Britain by Martins the Printers, Berwick Upon Tweed.

Introduction

What is Guided Reading?

Guided Reading is a valuable part of literacy work within the classroom, bridging the gap between shared and independent reading. A teacher usually works with a small group of children, who are of similar reading abilities, using a text that has been carefully selected to match the reading ability of the group.

The group setting naturally leads to discussion about the book. The teacher's role is to support pupils in their reading and discussion, and encourage them to respond to the text in a variety of different ways, including personal response. In Guided Reading children can put into practice the reading strategies that have been taught during Shared Reading sessions, and the teacher can monitor their progress more closely.

Aims of Guided Reading

With careful organisation and selection of appropriate texts, Guided Reading can:
- improve reading fluency;
- inspire confidence and promote enjoyment of reading;
- deepen understanding of texts;
- provide an opportunity for purposeful discussion, both teacher-led and spontaneous;
- provide a context for focused talk and listening, including role-play and drama activities;
- offer a stimulus for independent writing;
- provide an opportunity for the teacher to monitor the progress of individual children.

The main aim of Guided Reading sessions is to help children become independent readers.

Assessment

Guided Reading is an excellent opportunity to observe and assess the reading strategies used by individual children. When listening to individual children reading aloud, check for accuracy, fluency and understanding, and note the strategies they use to make sense of less familiar words.

The photocopiable record card on p. 42 may be used to record your observations about individual pupils within each group, noting particular strengths and needs. These observations may be used to help note progression and inform your assessment of children's reading development.

Ongoing assessment will also help you to identify when Guided Reading groups need to be reorganised. Children progress at different rates; those who are progressing more rapidly may benefit from reading more challenging texts, while children who are struggling may need opportunites to read more supportive texts.

How to organise Guided Reading

Many teachers find it helpful to organise daily, dedicated Guided Reading sessions to ensure an uninterrupted focus on the group. It works well if each session has a teaching sequence, and the suggestions in this guide offer a structure that you can draw on to make the most of each text and the learning opportunities within them.

Ideally, each group should have a session of Guided Reading every week. Other children in the class can be engaged in a variety of purposeful, independent activities, such as working on an activity relating to a previous Guided Reading session, carrying out reading journals, or paired reading with books of their own choice.

How to Use This Book

Teaching sequences

This guide outlines five teaching sequences to support the use of three Year 4 books with a Guided Reading group:

The Little Puppet Boy – for children who are inexperienced readers

The Story Thief – for children who have an average level of reading ability

The Hound of Ulster – for more experienced readers.

The teaching sequences take into account important elements of reading at Year 4. However, they will need to be adapted to take into consideration the specific needs of individual children within a group to ensure engagement and progress.

The teaching sequences have been planned to be approximately 30 minutes in length, although this will vary depending on how many of the ideas for "Returning to the text" you choose to include.

Independent reading

Each Guided Reading session is likely to be a combination of silent reading, reading aloud and discussion about the text, with the emphasis on reading for meaning. It will be important to hear all children read aloud at some point during the session in order to monitor their progress. However, less-experienced readers will probably need to spend more time reading aloud each session as they are likely to require a higher level of support developing fluency.

Fluency and understanding are both important in reading. Modelling how to read a sentence, with appropriate phrasing and expression, may help children to make sense of the text. Guided Reading offers many opportunities for word and sentence level work, but any significant difficulties demonstrated by individual children should be noted on the record card on p. 42 and addressed afterwards so as not to inhibit the group's understanding and enjoyment of the story.

Returning to the text

The questions and prompts in this section may be used to elicit children's understanding of the text. The questions can be asked either during reading or at the end of the chapter. It is not necessary to ask all the questions, as many of these will be covered in discussion arising spontaneously from reading the text. Encourage children to find the relevant parts of the text to support their answers and ask them to give reasons when offering opinions.

Experienced readers require less "literal" questioning and should be encouraged to develop higher order reading skills, for example prediction, inference and deduction.

Additional ideas for exploring the text further include:

- identifying features such as alliteration, similes, compound words, use of italics and capitalisation;
- opportunities for developing prediction skills;
- a range of role-play and drama activities;
- a stimulus for the activity sheet that follows.

It is important that groups have the experience of a reflective conversation about the book and not a "twenty questions" approach to test comprehension.

Next steps

The activity sheets may be used for independent work either in school or as homework. They offer a variety of ways for children to demonstrate their understanding of the stories, along with valuable opportunities for writing for different purposes.

Target Statements for Reading

The NLS target statements for reading at Year 4 will help inform your planning for progression in reading.

Word recognition and phonic knowledge:
- Use knowledge of word formation and a more extensive range of prefixes and suffixes to construct the meaning of words in context.

Grammatical awareness:
- Read aloud with intonation and expression taking account of punctuation, e.g. commas, dashes, hyphens.
- Use knowledge of how commas, connectives and full stops are used to join and separate clauses to maintain fluency and understanding when reading.
- Apply knowledge of the different uses of the apostrophe to maintain understanding.

Use of context:
- Understand narrative order and chronology, tracking the passing of time in stories.

Knowing how texts work:
- Understand how chapters and paragraphs are used to collect, order and build up ideas.

Interpretations and response: literary text:
- Identify and discuss issues locating evidence in the text.
- Interpret the effect the choice of language has – to create moods, build tension, etc.
- Identify the use of expressive, descriptive and figurative language in prose and poetry and interpret the effect of the choice of language to create mood, build tension, etc.
- Respond critically to issues raised in stories, locate evidence in text, and explore alternative courses of action and evaluate the author's solution.

Attitude:
- Develop different reading styles for different text types, e.g. sustained silent reading for longer fiction.
- Describe and review own reading habits.
- Take part in peer group discussion on books.

The Little Puppet Boy
by *James Riordan*

About the book

The Little Puppet Boy is a modern retelling of a well known tale from Russian folklore. The story recounts the adventures of Petroushka, a rag doll made by Lenochka and her grandmother. Petroushka was created to comfort the girl, and when Lenochka and her grandfather are travelling through the snow on a horse-drawn sleigh, it is Petroushka who saves them from hungry wolves by leaping from Lenochka's side and distracting the pack. He is later found by hunters, one of whom takes him home to his wife, who patches him up and gives him to a shop where he is purchased by a puppet master.

Petroushka the puppet clown makes his first appearance at an Easter Fair, where he stars alongside Strongman, Pretty Ballerina and Old Bones the Skeleton. He proves to be a great crowd-pleaser, but the little puppet boy isn't happy. He's had enough of making everyone laugh and wishes he were big and brave enough to challenge Strongman, who treats Pretty Ballerina so roughly. Petroushka wants to rescue Pretty Ballerina and take her away with him. Only a little girl at the front of the crowd is able to see that her favourite clown's grin conceals a broken heart.

Then Petroushka remembers how he saved Lenochka and decides that if he was brave enough to do that, he can stand up to Strongman. The following day, Petroushka rushes on stage and throws himself at Strongman. Strongman draws his sword and knocks Pretty Ballerina aside with his fist. Then he stabs Petroushka through the heart and the doll lies lifeless. But suddenly he appears on the tent top and dances high above the fair. He takes Pretty Ballerina in his arms, before flying away across the starry sky.

JAMES RIORDAN

Everyone turned round.

"Look," cried the little girl. "It's Petroushka. Hooray for Petroushka!"

Others took up her cry.

"Hooray for Petroushka! Hooray, hooray, hooray!"

The puppet master's mouth fell open. He stared from the broken doll in his hand to the real, live Petroushka on the tent top, laughing happily.

58

Old Bones's grin faded and he shuffled off into the cold night.

Even Strongman's face turned pale.

As for Pretty Ballerina, she smiled through her tears.

The children cheered and waved their hands.

59

The Little Puppet Boy:
Teaching Sequence 1

Summary of Chapter One

Lenochka is frightened hearing the wolves howl so her grandmother makes her a doll, which she names 'Petroushka'. The next day, Lenochka and her grandfather set off to see her mother, who is ill in hospital. A pack of wolves appear and Lenochka is afraid she will be dragged to the ground when, suddenly, Petroushka flies from her side, hitting the leader on the nose. The wolves tear at the rag doll, and Lenochka and her grandfather escape unharmed. Petroushka is found by hunters. One of them takes him home to his wife, who patches him up and gives him to a shop, where he is put on sale.

Teaching Sequence

Introduction
Talk about the book cover and read the blurb. Note that the synopsis ends with a question; why does the writer not give away the story ending?

Independent reading
Ask the group to read aloud Chapter One, focusing on reading for meaning.
- Help children with the pronunciation of the names *Lenochka* and *Petroushka*.
- Help children with less familiar words and phrases such as *sleigh* (p. 10), *gee-up* (p. 12), *pack* (p. 14), *destination* (p. 15), *narrow escape* (p. 17), *rouble* (p. 20).

Returning to the text
Develop children's understanding of the story by asking some of these questions either during reading or at the end of the chapter. Encourage them to find the relevant part in the text to support their answers.

1) What gives Lenochka's grandmother the idea to make a puppet? (Lenochka tells her she is scared and wants a doll to protect her (p. 8).)
2) What saved Lenochka and her grandfather from the wolves? (Petroushka flew from her side and hit the leader of the pack on the head. The pack stopped, thinking the doll was food (p. 14).)
3) What did the hunter's wife change abut Petroushka? (She gave him a cherry-red nose, a checked cap and painted freckles (p. 19).)
4) Why did the hunter's wife give Petroushka to a shop? (Because she had no children (p. 20).)

Talk about the setting for this story and ask children to point out phrases that refer to the features of the landscape, for example: *a lonely cottage, deep in the forest, giant fir trees, howling wolves*. What sort of mood does it help to create?

Look at the way the author describes the fir trees. Explain that the "waving arms" are branches. Discuss the effect of the language used.

What materials did Lenochka's grandmother use to make the puppet's hair, eyes and nose? (A mop, blue buttons and a carrot.) Discuss the steps that she would have taken to construct the doll. If the children were designing a doll like Petroushka, what materials would they use?

Point out the collective noun for wolves: "pack". Can the group think of other collective nouns for animals? For example: flock of sheep, litter of puppies, herd of cows, pride of lions.

Next steps
The children can now complete Activity Sheet 1: "How to Make a Rag Doll", which asks them to write instructions for making a rag doll like Petroushka.

How to Make a Rag Doll

Write instructions for making a rag doll like Petroushka.

You will need:

- _____
- _____
- _____
- _____
- _____

First _____

_____

_____

Next _____

_____

_____

Then _____

_____

_____

Finally _____

_____

_____

White Wolves Teachers' Resource
for Guided Reading Year 4
Stories From Different Cultures
© A & C Black 2007

The Little Puppet Boy:
Teaching Sequence 2

Summary of Chapter Two

A puppet master purchases Petroushka, and the clown makes his first appearance at an Easter Fair in St Petersburg. The curtains are parted to reveal Strongman in a desert. He sweeps up Pretty Ballerina in a wild dance. At the end of the dance, the curtains reopen to a snowy scene and Old Bones the Skeleton. He leaves to hisses and boos. Then Petroushka appears and, after falling flat on his face, he performs a Russian dance. The crowd laugh, not realising that their favourite clown's smile conceals a broken heart.

Teaching Sequence

Introduction
Recap on the events of the first chapter. What has happened to Petroushka so far?

Independent reading
Ask the group to read aloud Chapter Two, focusing on reading for meaning.
- Discuss less familiar words and phrases such as *St Petersburg, spick and span, sergeant, moustache* (p. 22), *shrieking, merry-go-round* (p. 23), *hustle and bustle* (p. 24), *a roll of drums* (p. 25), *Roll up! Roll up!, feats of strength* (p. 26), *theatre* (p. 29), *turban* (p. 30), *muscles, tutu, taffeta skirt, nursemaids* (p. 31), *applause, snowy plain* (p. 32), *beneath* (p. 35).

Returning to the text
Develop children's understanding of the story by asking some of these questions either during reading or at the end of the chapter. Encourage them to find the relevant part in the text to support their answers.
1) Why does the puppet master buy the rag doll? (He wants it to appear in his show; he thinks the children will love the clown's big grin and funny face (p. 21).)
2) What does the puppet master mean when he says of Old Bones the Skeleton: "He'll send chills up and down your spine" (p. 27)?
3) Beneath Petroushka's grin was a broken heart (p. 35). Why do you think the clown is so sad?

Reread pp. 22–24 and discuss how effectively the author has described the Easter Fair. Ask the children to pick out descriptions that convey the atmosphere. Note the alliterative phrases "spick and span" (p. 22), used to describe the smartly dressed soldiers, and "hustle and bustle" (p. 24), used to encapsulate the entire, busy scene.

Talk about the stereotyped characters: strong man, pretty ballerina, scary skeleton and funny clown. Look at how they are described. For example, the strongman is a giant figure with a turban on his head and curved sword at his belt (p. 30). Ask the children to locate the descriptions of the other characters. What other adjectives would they use to describe these characters? Discuss how Petroushka is unusual in that he is not a typical clown; his funny, smiling face hides sadness.

At the end of Chapter Two, Petroushka kicks up his heels in a Russian dance (p. 34). If possible, show the group a video clip of Russian dancing. Alternatively, show a picture of a Russian dancer in national costume.

Next steps
The children can now complete Activity Sheet 2: "Showtime", which asks children to design a poster advertising the puppet master's show and introducing the stars who appear in it.

Showtime

Design a poster advertising the puppet show at the Easter Fair.

- State where the show will be performed.
- Briefly describe what the show is about.
- Introduce the stars of the show and draw pictures of them, if you like.

White Wolves Teachers' Resource
for Guided Reading Year 4
Stories From Different Cultures
© A & C Black 2007

The Little Puppet Boy:
Teaching Sequence 3

Summary of Chapter Three

The crowd draw back in fear as Strongman seizes Pretty Ballerina and throws her in the air, before whirling her around in a wild dance. Petroushka stands in the wings and a little girl in the crowd sees the love in his eyes for Pretty Ballerina. Petroushka believes he is too weak and lacking in courage to be noticed by Pretty Ballerina. Then he remembers how he saved Lenochka from the wolves and decides that if he was brave enough to do that, he can stand up to Strongman.

Teaching Sequence

Introduction
Ask the children to remind you of the characters who appear in the puppet show. What can they remember about each of them? Why is the little clown unhappy?

Independent reading
Ask the group to read aloud Chapter Three, focusing on reading for meaning.
- Discuss less familiar words and phrases such as *interval*, *sweet cockerel on a stick* (p. 36), *challenge*, *seized* (p. 38), *whirled*, *blur*, *murmured* (p. 39), *vow*, *duel* (p. 43).

Returning to the text
Develop children's understanding of the story by asking some of these questions either during reading or at the end of the chapter. Encourage them to find the relevant part in the text to support their answers.
1) How do the crowd react to Strongman? (They are afraid of him. Women and children draw back in fear and "even the soldiers seemed scared of his fierce looks" (p. 38).)
2) How does Strongman treat Pretty Ballerina?

(He treats her roughly; he throws her up in the air and whirls her round and round (pp. 38–39).)
3) What does the little girl notice about Petroushka? (She sees the love in his eyes for Pretty Ballerina and how sad he looks (p. 39).)
4) Why does Petroushka think Pretty Ballerina won't take any notice of him? (He sees himself as "only a rag doll, a clown who makes people laugh". He believes she is too beautiful and he is "too weak and not brave at all" (p. 42).)

Talk about what it is that changes Petroushka's mind and makes him vow to challenge Strongman to a duel. (He remembers how he saved a little girl from the wolves and concludes that, if he was brave enough to do that, he can stand up to Strongman (p. 43).) This thought process provides a link between this part of the story and the earlier stage in the little puppet boy's journey.

Point out that it is a little girl who notices the sadness in Petroushka's eyes and sees his love for Pretty Ballerina. Can the group think of other stories in which a child notices something that others around them haven't, for example, the child who sees that the Emperor is not wearing any clothes in *The Emperor's New Clothes*.

In pairs, children could pretend to be Petroushka and the little girl. They could discuss why the clown feels unhappy, and the little girl could make suggestions about how he could make his feelings known to Pretty Ballerina, and how to stand up to Strongman.

Next steps
Activity Sheet 3: "Journey to St Petersburg" asks children to recount, in sequence, the events that have happened in Petroushka's short life.

Journey to St Petersburg

Think about the long journey Petroushka has made in his short life.

Write about the sequence of events that have happened along the way. Use the illustrations to help you remember the order in which they happened.

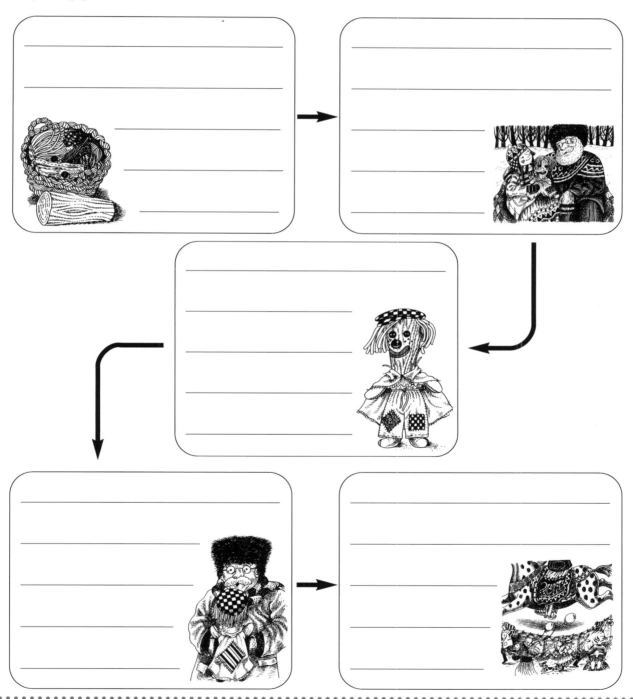

White Wolves Teachers' Resource
for Guided Reading Year 4
Stories From Different Cultures
© A & C Black 2007

The Little Puppet Boy:
Teaching Sequence 4

Summary of Chapter Four

The following day, the little girl and her mother are at the front of the show again. Petroushka is watching from the wings. Old Bones creeps up behind him and points out how scared Pretty Ballerina looks. Petroushka needs no further encouragement; he rushes on stage and throws himself at Strongman. Strongman draws his sword, ready to attack, but Pretty Ballerina throws herself between them. Strongman knocks her aside with his fist and she screams at Petroushka to run.

Teaching Sequence

Introduction
Recap briefly on the events of Chapter Three. What does Petroushka intend to do next? What do the group think the outcome will be if Strongman takes up the challenge?

Independent reading
Ask the group to read aloud Chapter Four, focusing on reading for meaning.
• Discuss less familiar words and phrases such as *unaware, wings, unexpected* (p. 45), *clutches* (p. 46), *aside, glee* (p. 49).

Returning to the text
Develop children's understanding of the story by asking some of these questions either during reading or at the end of the chapter. Encourage them to find the relevant part in the text to support their answers.
1) What finally provoked Petroushka to rush on stage and throw himself at Strongman? (Old Bones, who was "doing all he could to cause a fight" (p. 46).)
2) How did the crowd react to the fighting? (There was a mixed reaction. Part of it "looked on in

horror" while others cheered, thinking that it was all part of the show (p. 50).)
3) Why didn't the puppet master step in and break up the fight? (He saw no reason to worry, as long as the fight was bringing in a crowd (p. 51).)

Talk about the change in Petroushka's attitude and new-found strength of character. Ask children to find references in the text. For example, the author uses language such as "determined", "mighty effort", "staring", "made up his mind", "waiting for his chance" (p. 45).

Look at the way the author describes Strongman's body language: "Strongman rolled his eyes, puffed out his chest and drew his long, curved sword" (p. 48). What does this tell us about him? (For example, rolling his eyes could be a sign of exasperation, or he could be rolling his eyes in disbelief at Petroushka's bold declaration to teach him a lesson; puffing out his chest makes him appear large and intimidating; drawing his sword is threatening behaviour – a sign of aggression.) Children could model Strongman's body language to illustrate these points.

Discuss the character of Old Bones, who, we are told, "hopped up and down with glee" when the fight broke out. What motivates him? Is he really evil? Children could explore the skeleton's character further by re-enacting the scene at the beginning of the chapter when Old Bones tries to provoke Petroushka into attacking Strongman and saving Pretty Ballerina.

Next steps
The children can now complete Activity Sheet 4: "The Good, the Bad and the Ugly", which asks them to compile detailed profiles of three of the characters in the puppet show.

The Good, the Bad and the Ugly

Write a profile of each of the characters below.

Think about:
- Their physical appearance
- Their role in the show
- What motivates them?
- What are their strengths / weaknesses?

Petroushka

_____
_____
_____
_____
_____

Strongman

_____
_____
_____
_____
_____

Old Bones

_____
_____
_____
_____
_____

White Wolves Teachers' Resource
for Guided Reading Year 4
Stories From Different Cultures
© A & C Black 2007

The Little Puppet Boy:
Teaching Sequence 5

Summary of Chapter Five

Strongman flies into a rage and stabs Petroushka through the heart with his sword. Pretty Ballerina screams and falls down beside him. Just as it seems that nothing will save him, the little girl in the crowd spots Petroushka on the tent top, laughing happily. The puppet master stares in disbelief at the broken doll in his hand while the real, live Petroushka swoops down to take Pretty Ballerina in his arms and fly away.

Teaching Sequence

Introduction
Discuss Petroushka's fate at the end of Chapter Four when we are told that "nothing could save the little clown". Ask the group to predict how the story will end. Is there any hope for Petroushka?

Independent reading
Ask the group to read aloud Chapter Five, focusing on reading for meaning.
- Discuss less familiar words and phrases such as *thrust*, *lifeless* (p. 53), *uncertainly* (p. 54), *north wind* (p. 55).

Returning to the text
Develop children's understanding of the story by asking some of these questions either during reading or at the end of the chapter. Encourage them to find the relevant part in the text to support their answers.
1) Why was Strongman in such a rage at the beginning of the chapter? (He was angry that the clown had hit him (p. 52).)
2) How do the crowd react to Strongman's threatening behaviour? (The women and children fear for Petroushka and yell at him to run (p. 52); the men cheer with approval (p. 53).)

3) How does Old Bones react when he sees Petroushka laughing on the tent top? (He stops smiling and shuffles away (p. 59), it is as though he is disappointed by the happy outcome.)

Talk about the theme of strength versus weakness. Discuss how strength can refer to both body and mind. Strongman is physically stronger than Petroushka, but Petroushka demonstrates how strength of spirit can be more powerful.

Talk about Petroushka's love for Pretty Ballerina. He is motivated by love, and love proves to be a powerful force in this story. What motivates the other characters? For example, greed motivates the puppet master, vanity motivates Strongman.

How does Pretty Ballerina feel towards Petroushka? Ask the children to find evidence in the text to support their views. For example, she screams when Strongman stabs Petroushka, and falls down beside him (p. 53); she smiles through her tears when she sees him on the tent top (p. 58).

Talk about the line, "It's only make believe, isn't it?" (p. 54). Discuss how the boundaries between make believe and reality are blurred in this story. For example, the crowd react to the puppets in the show as though they are real.

Ask the group what they think about the way the story ends. Does it remind them of any other stories? For example, *Pinocchio*, in which a puppet boy changes into a real boy.

Next steps
The children can now complete Activity Sheet 5: "Through the Eyes of a Little Girl", which asks them to write what happened at the puppet show from perspective of the little girl.

Through the Eyes of a Little Girl

Imagine you are the little girl watching the puppet show with your mother. Write about what you saw on the second day of the show.

Mama and I returned to the fair today because I wanted to see the puppet show again. I wanted to see poor little Petroushka. We stood at the front, just like yesterday. But today something was wrong. The red velvet curtains opened and the desert dance began, just like before, but then something unexpected happened…

_____

_____

_____

_____

_____

_____

_____

_____

_____

_____

White Wolves Teachers' Resource
for Guided Reading Year 4
Stories From Different Cultures
© A & C Black 2007

The Story Thief by Andrew Fusek Peters

About the book

The Story Thief is a well known tale from African folklore. Nyame the sky god has a special treasure; all the stories ever told are held in a big, brass chest at the end of his bed. Anansi, the cleverest of spiders, sees that the people down on Earth are bored, so she makes a ladder that reaches up into the sky, determined to take possession of the stories. Nyame agrees, but only if Anansi succeeds in completing a series of "impossible" tasks.

The first task is to capture Mmoboro, "a tribe of hornets with stings that make you swell like a balloon". She manages to do this by tricking the queen and trapping the hornets inside a coconut.

The second is to capture Osebo the leopard. Anansi does this by luring him into a game of "tie-you-up" with flattery and dishonesty.

The final task is the trickiest of all. Anansi must capture Mmoatia, the invisible fairy. Anansi achieves this by tempting the sweet-toothed fairy into a sticky trap, using a sugar-coated clay monkey, and a bowl of porridge and honey.

Anansi then drags a knapsack containing her victims up the ladder to Nyame's door. At first, Nyame does not believe Anansi and foolishly asks her to prove she has completed the tasks. Anansi releases Mmoboro the angry tribe of hornets and Osebo the leopard with his terrifying roar. Nyame, desperate to be free, begs and pleads to be spared. Finally, Mmoatia the invisible fairy grabs Nyame, and dances him out of his room and across the sky. Anansi pushes Nyame's treasure chest through the clouds and the words and stories inside it spill out across the land. The people on Earth are never bored again.

The leopard rolled his eyes as if the whole thing was too much. But secretly he was very excited. "Go on then. What game shall we play? I'm all ears."

"Well…" Anansi tried to look like she was thinking deeply. Then suddenly her eyes lit up. "How about the tie-you-up game?"

"Never heard of it. Is it fun? I could do with a bit of fun."

"It's so funny, the tears will be rolling down your face, I promise!" said Anansi. "The game goes like this. I roll over and you tie me up. Then you untie me. You roll over and I tie you up. Then I untie you. Whoever makes the best knots wins the game!"

"Hmmm…" said Osebo, suspiciously. "It's a very strange kind of game."

30

31

The Story Thief: Teaching Sequence 1

Summary of Chapter One

Nyame, the sky god, has a brass chest containing a bag filled with the words, dreams and ideas of every story ever told. Meanwhile, down on Earth, people are bored with no stories to tell. Anansi, the cleverest of spiders, decides to do something about this. She spins a ladder up into the sky, knocks on Nyame's door and demands the bag of stories. Nyame sets her a series of challenges. Anansi bravely accepts and vows to return the next day. Nyame laughs at the spider's determination; the tasks he has set are impossible and he does not believe she stands a chance.

Teaching Sequence

Introduction
Talk about the book cover and read the blurb. Point out that this story is a well known tale from Africa. Look at the illustration on the front cover and ask the children to identify the characters Nyame and Anansi.

Independent reading
Ask the group to read aloud Chapter One, focusing on reading for meaning.
- Help children with the pronunciation of the names *Nyame*, *Anansi*, *Mmoboro*, *Osebo* and *Mmoatia*.
- Help children with less familiar words and phrases such as *tantrum* (p. 8), *possession* (p. 9), *soothe* (p. 10), *villains* (p. 11), *scuttled*, *calabash shells* (p. 12), *spin yarn* (p. 13), *stuttered* (p. 15), *tribe of hornets*, *easy-peasy* (p. 16).

Returning to the text
Develop children's understanding of the story by asking some of these questions either during reading or at the end of the chapter. Encourage them to find the relevant part in the text to support their answers.

1) How is the character Nyame described? (He is presented as the "most bad-tempered god anyone has ever seen" (p. 7). The text refers to *tantrums*, *complaining*, *tears*, *growls* and *grumbles* (p. 9).)
2) How do Nyame's moods affect the people on Earth? (His moods control the weather; anger causes thunder and lightning and his tears cause rain to fall (p. 8); when he is happy, "a smile like the sun" lights up his face (p. 9).)
3) What does Nyame keep in the chest at the bottom of his bed? (The words, dreams and ideas that made up every story ever told (p. 9).)
4) How does Nyame respond to Anansi's demand? (He seems angry and he roars at her (p. 15), but he also seems to admire Anansi's bravery and therefore does not harm her. (p. 17).)

Chapter one is full of similes. How many can the children identify? For example, "a smile like the sun" (p. 9), "minds as empty as calabash shells", "we are like rivers run dry" (p. 12), "swell like a balloon" (p. 16). Discuss the meaning of each. Ask a child to find a picture of a calabash shell on the Internet and find out where they originate from.

Talk about the descriptions of stories on p. 11. Can the group think of stories they have read with "princes to fall in love with", "villains to outwit" and "happy-ever-afters"? What sort of stories do they enjoy most?

Talk about the small spider's bravery in approaching the thunderous sky god, and demanding his most prized possession. She declares Nyame's challenges "easy-peasy" (p. 16); does she realise that she is being tricked and that Nyame has set her impossible tasks?

Next steps
The children can now complete Activity Sheet 1: "Impossible!", which asks them to describe the tasks that Nyame has set for Anansi and invent another impossible task of their own.

Impossible!

Describe the tasks that Nyame set Anansi in your own words. What challenges will the spider need to overcome?

Task one: _____   Challenge: _____

_____   _____

_____   _____

Task two: _____   Challenge: _____

_____   _____

_____   _____

Task three: _____   Challenge: _____

_____   _____

_____   _____

Now invent an impossible task of your own.

_____

_____

_____

_____

_____

The Story Thief: Teaching Sequence 2

Summary of Chapter Two

Anansi puzzles over how to tackle the impossible task of capturing a whole tribe of hornets. She decides to carve a hole in a coconut, which she fills with water and seals with a cork plug. Then she carries the coconut to the top of the tree where the hornets are sleeping, empties the water into their nest and hides as the angry hornets pour out of the hive. Anansi feigns sympathy and offers the coconut as a new home. As the last hornet flies in, Anansi replaces the plug, trapping them. She tucks the coconut into her knapsack and sets off to tackle the second challenge.

Teaching Sequence

Introduction
Recap on the events of the first chapter. Which of the challenges set by Nyame do the group think will prove most difficult and why?

Independent reading
Ask the group to read aloud Chapter Two, focusing on reading for meaning.
- Discuss less unfamiliar words and phrases such as *capture* (p. 18), *knapsack, plucked, carved* (p. 19), *snooze, hive* (p. 20), *salute, invisible* (p. 22), *cradle, commanded* (p. 24).

Returning to the text
Develop children's understanding of the story by asking some of these questions either during reading or at the end of the chapter. Encourage them to find the relevant part in the text to support their answers.
1) What does Anansi use to trap the hornets? (A coconut, which she seals with a cork plug.)
2) How did Anansi get the hornets to leave their hive? (She flooded their nest with water (p. 21).)
3) Is Anansi afraid of Mmoboro? (Yes. When the hornets pour out of their hive, buzzing angrily, Anansi wants to run away (p. 21).)
4) How does Anansi convince the queen to fly into the coconut trap? (She flatters the queen and fakes sympathy: "my heart felt heavy when I thought you might lose your home" (p. 23).)

Note the elegant way in which Anansi addresses Mmoboro: "Oh, great and graceful Mmoboro, whose stings are as savage as spears, I salute you" (p. 22). Can children spot the alliteration and simile in this sentence? How does the queen hornet respond? Can the children find any other similes in Chapter Two? For example, "Mmoboro… whose stings make you swell like a balloon" (p. 25).

Notice how formally Anansi and the queen behave towards one another. The queen bows gracefully before Anansi (p. 23). In turn, Anansi addresses the queen as "Dear queen" (p. 24).

Discuss how Anansi shows that she can in fact spin a yarn when she tells Mmoboro that the rains have come and flooded her hive. Anansi spins a web of deceit, telling Mmoboro that her heart felt heavy at the thought of the queen losing her home.

If possible, show the group a real coconut. Drain the milk by pushing a skewer into the three holes at the top. The coconut's shell can be broken by placing it inside a polythene bag and hitting it with a hammer on a hard surface. The children may be surprised at how hard the shell is.

Next steps
The children can now complete Activity Sheet 2: "Similes with Bite!", which asks them to create similes and compare their ideas with those used in Chapters One and Two.

Similes with Bite!

In Chapter Two, Anansi captures "Mmoboro, the tribe of hornets whose stings make you swell like a balloon".

The author's description of Mmoboro includes a simile. Underline the simile.

Remember:

- A simile is when two things are compared that share a similar feature.
- A word such as "like" or "as" is used to compare them. For example: "as cold as ice" or "like a fish out of water".

Think of an interesting way to complete each of the following similes.

Without stories, the people's minds are as empty as

_____

With no ideas or dreams or tales, they are like

_____

Mmoboro are a tribe of hornets, whose stings are as savage as

_____

Their stings make you swell like

_____

Osebo is a leopard with teeth like

_____

Look at Chapters One and Two and find similes used by the author. How do they compare with your similes?

White Wolves Teachers' Resource
for Guided Reading Year 4
Stories From Different Cultures
© A & C Black 2007

The Story Thief: Teaching Sequence 3

Summary of Chapter Three

Osebo the leopard is more terrifying than the tribe of hornets. However, Anansi intends to outwit him with another clever plan. She lures him into a game of "tie you up", and suggests that, since he will obviously win, he should be tied up first so that they can get Anansi's turn over and done with. Osebo enters into the spirit of the game, admitting that he is actually quite impressed at the spider's knots. At this point, Anansi reveals that she has tricked Osebo. She pulls him into her knapsack and sets off to tackle the final challenge.

Teaching Sequence

Introduction
Talk about the character of Anansi. What qualities has she revealed about herself so far? Does she appear capable of overcoming the challenges that Nyame has set?

Independent reading
Ask the group to read aloud Chapter Three, focusing on reading for meaning.
- Discuss less familiar words and phrases such as *hovered* (p. 23), *mighty-fanged*, *compliment* (p. 28), *suspiciously* (p. 31), *lightning-limbed*, *obviously*, *insist* (p. 33), *pouted* (p. 35), *wailed* (p. 36).
- Talk about the wordplay on p. 27 relating to the homophone "game". Check that the group understand both definitions of this word.
- Point out how Anansi uses another homophone (knot / not) for humorous effect when she jokes, "I'm afraid knot!" (p. 35).

Returning to the text
Develop children's understanding of the story by asking some of these questions either during reading or at the end of the chapter. Encourage them to find the relevant part in the text to support their answers.

1) How does Osebo pass the time? (He counts his spots, flicks flies with his tail and hunts game (p. 27).)
2) Is Anansi afraid of Osebo? (Yes, when he yawns, Osebo reveals a set of very sharp teeth (p. 28), which causes Anansi to reflect that this challenge is "far worse than the hornets".)
3) What does Anansi mean when she promises Osebo, "the tears will be rolling down your face" (p. 31)? (Her words have a double meaning: Osebo believes she is referring to tears of laughter, however Anansi is speaking literally; Osebo will be crying tears of distress.)

Notice how the author often chooses words for their effect. For example, he uses alliteration when referring to Osebo's huge "padded paws" (p. 29) and describes him as "lightning-limbed" (p. 33). Ask the group to identify other adjectives and phrases used to describe Osebo, for example: *proud, mighty-fanged, clever, rather stupid*. Make a list and ask the group to identify which of the descriptions are used by the narrator and which are used by Anansi. Are all of the descriptions accurate? Point out that Anansi often praises her victims but does not always mean what she says.

Talk about the different expressions that are included in Chapter Three. For example, most animals "steered well clear" of Osebo (p. 27); Osebo tells Anansi, "I'm all ears" (p. 30); Anansi tells the leopard, "Once we start and you get the hang of it, time will fly by!" (p. 32). What do the expressions mean and what quality do they add to the narrative?

Next steps
Activity Sheet 3: "Anansi, the Kindest and Cleverest of Spiders?" asks children to think about the character of Anansi and consider different aspects of her personality as revealed in the story so far.

Anansi, the Kindest and Cleverest of Spiders?

Look at the adjectives below. They describe the character of Anansi at different points in the story. Look back at the first three chapters and find examples in the text to illustrate each adjective.

dishonest

"I'm not very good at tying knots..."

_____

clever _____

_____

brave _____

_____

kind _____

_____

What other adjectives would you use to describe Anansi? Can you find quotes in the text to illustrate them?

_____

_____

_____

_____

White Wolves Teachers' Resource
for Guided Reading Year 4
Stories From Different Cultures
© A & C Black 2007

The Story Thief: Teaching Sequence 4

Summary of Chapter Four

Anansi approaches the final "impossible" task with a sense of defeat. But after much thought, she sets about carving a monkey's body from clay and coats it with sticky molasses. She places a bowl of porridge and honey in the monkey's lap, she pushes a clay monkey's head onto a stick and, hidden from view, attempts to entice Mmoatia the invisible fairy into her trap. The smell of porridge lures Mmoatia, but she is angered by the monkey's silence. She strikes him on the shoulder and her hand sticks fast. As she tries to pull herself away, her other hand becomes stuck. She kicks the monkey and, very quickly, finds herself trapped. With the fairy safe inside her knapsack, Anansi sets off to reveal her conquests to the sky god.

Teaching Sequence

Introduction

Recap briefly on the events of the story so far. What challenges has Anansi overcome? Do the children think Anansi will successfully complete the third and final challenge, to capture Mmoatia the invisible fairy?

Independent reading

Ask the group to read aloud Chapter Four, focusing on reading for meaning.
- Discuss less familiar words and phrases such as *porridge*, (p. 38), *raided, larder, molasses, sculpture, drizzled* (p. 40), *source* (p. 41), *ate her fill* (p. 43), *insulting, address* (p. 44), *brute, stomach* (p. 45), *favour, bundled* (p. 47).

Returning to the text

Develop children's understanding of the story by asking some of these questions either during reading or at the end of the chapter. Encourage them to find the relevant part in the text to support their answers.

1) What motivates Anansi to continue with the tasks and take on the final, seemingly impossible, challenge? (She thinks of all the miserable people who have no stories (p. 37).)
2) What "fact" had Anansi been told about fairies? (A wise man had told her that they love to eat porridge, especially with honey (p. 38).)
3) What clues alert Anansi to the invisible fairy's presence? (Anansi can hear Mmoatia's rumbling tummy (p. 42). She hears Mmoatia addressing the monkey and she sees the spoon rise up in the air as Mmoatia tastes the porridge (p. 43).)

"Anansi's final task was the hardest" (p. 37). In what way is this task more difficult than the previous tasks?

What do we learn about the character of Mmoatia? The way she addresses the monkey tells us about her personality. She seems friendly to begin with, wishing the monkey a good day and asking him politely if he will share the porridge, "please". However, she grows impatient when the monkey does not speak and quickly loses her temper, striking him on the shoulder. When she becomes stuck, she drops her polite manner and tries to kick the monkey, yelling "Let go of me, you brute!" (p. 45).

Talk about the theme of trickery that runs through this story. Mmoatia, like Osebo, cries out, "You tricked me! It's not fair!" (p. 36 and p. 46). Discuss with the group whether Anansi's actions are justifiable. Talk about her motivation for capturing Mmoatia and Osebo. Is she justified in tricking them if she is acting in the interests of others, for a greater good?

Next steps

The children can now complete Activity Sheet 4: "A Mean Trick!", which asks them to write about events from Mmoatia's perspective.

A Mean Trick!

Imagine you are Mmoatia the invisible fairy. How would you feel about being tricked?

Write what happened to you and describe how you feel about it.

It was a mean trick, tempting me with my favourite food. The porridge smelled so delightful it made my nose twitch. And I was feeling so hungry that my tummy rumbled like thunder!

_____

_____

_____

_____

_____

_____

_____

_____

_____

_____

_____

_____

White Wolves Teachers' Resource
for Guided Reading Year 4
Stories From Different Cultures
© A & C Black 2007

The Story Thief: Teaching Sequence 5

Summary of Chapter Five

Anansi drags the knapsack up into the clouds and knocks at Nyame's door. At first, Nyame does not believe it when she tells him she has brought what he asked for and asks her to prove it. Anansi undoes the knapsack, releasing the tribe of hornets who, believing that Nyame is to blame for their entrapment, sting him in revenge. Then Osebo the leopard tumbles out. Nyame begs Osebo not to hurt him. He flatters Osebo, who finally backs off and slides back to Earth down Anansi's web. Finally, Mmoatia the invisible fairy grabs Nyame and dances him right out of his room. Anansi pushes Nyame's treasure chest through the clouds and the words inside spill out across the land.

Teaching Sequence

Introduction
Talk about the ways in which Anansi has managed to overcome the challenges set by Nyame. How will the story end? Will Nyame hand over the treasure chest of stories to Anansi?

Independent reading
Ask the group to read aloud Chapter Five, focusing on reading for meaning.
- Discuss less familiar words and phrases such as *prove* (p. 49), *agony*, *revenge* (p. 50), *decisions*, *scrawny* (p. 53), *stalked* (p. 55), *shove* (p. 58), *fluttered*, *seedlings* (p. 60).
- Check that the children understand the wordplay on p. 54, when Nyame addresses Osebo as "prince of purr-fection".

Returning to the text
Develop children's understanding of the story by asking some of these questions either during reading or at the end of the chapter. Encourage them to find the relevant part in the text to support their answers.

1) How does Nyame respond when Anansi tells him she has brought what he asked for? (He does not believe her and asks for proof (p. 49).)
2) Why do the hornets attack Nyame? (Anansi has told them that Nyame was to blame for their entrapment; it is an act of revenge (p. 50).)
3) How does Nyame escape the sharp fangs of Osebo? (He begs Osebo not to hurt him (p. 52). He flatters Osebo (p. 54).)
4) What happens to Nyame at the end of the story? Mmoatia grabs him and dances him right out of his room. To this day, they are still dancing (pp. 56–57).)

Talk about the themes of weather and the elements. Ask the children to look for references in the text. For example, when Anansi knocks at Nyame's door: "'Go away!' thundered the sky god." (p. 49); "Osebo took one look at Nyame and roared louder than any storm." (p. 52).

Point out the humour that is woven into the story, particularly in the chapters that feature Osebo the leopard. Ask the children to talk about the lines that amuse them most.

Discuss Anansi's behaviour in the story. In what ways is her behaviour typical of a spider? For example, feeding on dried-up fly (p. 18). In what ways is her behaviour unlike that of a spider? Discuss how the author presents realistic animal characters, but also gives them human characteristics for the purposes of the story.

The children could explore different scenes from the story through drama, re-enacting Anansi's interactions with the various characters in pairs.

Next steps
The children can now complete Activity Sheet 5: "Words that Tell Stories", which focuses on the adjectives used to describe the main characters.

Words that Tell Stories

These are all adjectives that describe the characters in *The Story Thief*.

Link the adjectives to the characters they describe. Some of the words may describe more than one character.

Anansi

bad-tempered

clever

brave

selfish

angry

stupid   great

bored

little

greedy

handsome

graceful

lightning-limbed

kind

proud

Nyame

Mmoboro

Mmoatia

Osebo

Add adjectives of your own and link them to the characters they describe.

White Wolves Teachers' Resource
for Guided Reading Year 4
Stories From Different Cultures
© A & C Black 2007

The Hound of Ulster
by *Malachy Doyle*

About the book

The Hound of Ulster is a traditional Irish tale. From an early age, Setanta dreams of becoming a Red Branch Knight, one of the king's warriors. One day, when he accompanies his father to market, Setanta sees the king's boys practising their hurling skills and he runs to join them, hoping to prove to the king that he is good enough to become a warrior. The king is impressed by the small boy's determination and ability. He invites Setanta to join him at the feast of Culann the blacksmith and considers allowing Setanta to join his band of warriors on condition that he agrees to being looked after by the other boys. Setanta tells the king he will join him only after he has fought the boys and proved himself worthy to serve the king.

At the banquet, the king's host asks if it is safe to let his ferocious guard dog loose. The king, whose mind is on the feast, confirms that all his men are safely inside the house, so Culann orders that his dog be set free. When Setanta, victorious from defeating the young warriors, approaches Culann's house, he finds the gate locked. As he climbs over the wall, the "fearsome hound" lunges towards him. Setanta acts instinctively, and kills the beast.

The king and his men are cheered that Setanta is alive, but Culann the blacksmith is not happy. Without the guard dog, he cannot keep his family safe. Setanta offers to take the dog's place and guard the blacksmith's house and land until he can find another. The king approves of this plan, promising to find and train another dog for Culann. Setanta is awarded the name of "Cuchulainn, the Hound of Culann" as a mark of his courage and strength.

"I would be pleased to do so," replied the king, much to the blacksmith's delight. "I shall come tomorrow."

On the way to Culann's house the following morning, King Conor stopped by the green to watch his young warriors at play. He was surprised, though, as the ball rose high into the air, to see a strange boy, much smaller than the rest, rushing on to the field.

With incredible skill for one so young, Setanta caught the ball on the edge of his stick, dodged round the others, slipped it past them and scored a wonderful goal.

18

19

The Hound of Ulster: Teaching Sequence 1

Summary of Chapter One

Setanta's ambition is to become a Red Branch Knight. His family tell him only sons of noblemen become warriors but Setanta does not abandon his dream. Instead, he practises his skills at games and sports. One night, Setanta asks his father to let him accompany him to the market in Emain Macha. When they arrive in the town, Setanta sees the king's boys practising their skills and he runs to join them, believing that now is the time to prove that the son of a shepherd is good enough to become a warrior and serve the king.

Teaching Sequence

Introduction

Talk about the book cover and read the blurb. Does the cover artwork give any clues about the type of story that this will be? Point out that it is a traditional tale from Ireland. Check that the children understand what a hound is.

Independent reading

Ask the group to read aloud Chapter One, focusing on reading for meaning.
- Help children with the pronunciation of the names *Setanta*, *Conor Mac Nessa* and *Culann*.
- Help with the pronunciation of the place names *Ulster* and *Emain Macha*.
- Help children with less familiar words and phrases such as *nobleman*, *warriors*, *shepherd* (p. 8), *headquarters*, *champions*, *hurley stick*, *javelin* (p. 9), *rascal* (p. 11), *whoop*, *holler* (p. 14).

Returning to the text

Develop children's understanding of the story by asking some of these questions either during reading or at the end of the chapter. Encourage them to find the relevant part in the text to support their answers.
1) What reasons does Setanta's mother give against

him becoming a Red Branch Knight? (She says that he is too young, too skinny and too poor (p. 7); only the sons of noblemen become warriors (p. 8).)
2) How do Setanta's parents address him? (They refer to him as "child", "love", or "boy"; they do not use his name.)
3) Why does Setanta spend so much time practising hurling and other sports? (He wants to be as good as the Red Branch Knights, who are chosen for their skills at games and sports (p. 9).)

Talk about the way the author opens the story: Setanta always knew that he was different. Discuss the effect of immediately placing the focus on Setanta and indicating that he is an unusual character.

How many children are familiar with the game of hurling? What can they tell you about it? (It is a game similar to hockey; players use a curved, wooden stick called a hurley to catch and throw the ball.)

By the end of the chapter, do the group share Setanta's mother's opinion that her son is too young, skinny and poor to become a Red Branch Knight? What qualities has he displayed so far?

The children could re-enact the scene where Setanta tries to persuade his father to let him accompany him to market. Discuss how this scene is relevant today; how many children can recall trying to persuade a parent or guardian to let them do something?

Next steps

The children can now complete Activity Sheet 1: "Impossible Dream?", which asks them to consider reasons for and against Setanta pursuing his dream of becoming a Red Branch Knight.

Impossible Dream?

Setanta dreams of becoming a Red Branch Knight. What are the chances of his dream becoming a reality?

Reread Chapter One and look for reasons for and against Setanta becoming a Red Branch Knight. List them in the table below.

For	Against
■ It's something Setanta really wants to do.	■ He's too young.
■ _____	■ _____
■ _____	■ _____
■ _____	■ _____
■ _____	■ _____

Should Setanta chase his dream or should he forget it and concentrate on becoming a shepherd like his father?

_____

_____

_____

_____

_____

_____

White Wolves Teachers' Resource
for Guided Reading Year 4
Stories From Different Cultures
© A & C Black 2007

The Hound of Ulster: Teaching Sequence 2

Summary of Chapter Two

On his way to dine with the blacksmith Culann, Conor Mac Nessa stops at the green to watch his young warriors at play. He notices Setanta and is impressed. His young warriors, however, are angry with the uninvited stranger, who is showing them up in front of their lord and master. They try everything they can to take the ball away from him, but to no avail. Eventualy, the tallest of the warriors picks up his spear, and it looks as though Setanta might be killed then and there, but for "a great cry, splitting the air".

Teaching Sequence

Introduction
Recap on the events of the first chapter. How do the group think the king's boys will react when Setanta joins them, intent on proving he has the potential to become a warrior?

Independent reading
Ask the group to read aloud Chapter Two, focusing on reading for meaning.
- Discuss less familiar words and phrases such as *wealth*, *blacksmith* (p. 17), *lord and master* (p. 20), *intruder*, *advantage* (p. 21), *slow-footed* (p. 22), *duck* (p. 24).

Returning to the text
Develop children's understanding of the story by asking some of these questions either during reading or at the end of the chapter. Encourage them to find the relevant part in the text to support their answers.
1) What do the king's people think of him? (He is "greatly loved by all" because he spends time getting to know his people (p. 16).)
2) Where was the king going when he stopped at the green to watch his young warriors? (He was going to visit the blacksmith Culann.)

3) Why were the young warriors angry with Setanta? (Because he had joined their game uninvited and he was showing them up in front of the king (p. 20).)
4) What skills did Setanta demonstrate on the field? (He was faster than anyone else; his small size enabled him to dash between the other players' legs; he never lost possession of the ball; he never missed a goal and, when he was put in goal, he stopped every shot (pp. 21–22).)

Notice how Setanta is referred to in Chapter Two: *strange boy, child, intruder, shepherd's boy, the stranger, farmer's boy*. As in the previous chapter, his name is never used except by the narrator. He is a stranger with no identity.

Look at the words spoken by the leader of the king's warriors: "You can't just parade on to the field and join in our game without even asking. It is an insult to us and to the king!" What do the group think about this point of view? Is there any truth in what he says? Is Setanta insulting either the warriors or the king? Is that his intention?

Discuss whether the group feel any sympathy towards the young warriors. Talk about the relevance of this scene to young readers today. Have they ever tried to join in a game and found that they were not welcome? How did they feel?

If possible, show the group a video clip of a game of hurling. Talk about the skills needed to play the game.

Next steps
The children can now complete Activity Sheet 2: "Who Do You Think You Are?", which asks them to think about what the king's young warriors might say to Setanta after being humiliated by him on the field. Encourage them to refer back to the text for ideas.

Who Do You Think You Are?

What do you think the king's band of warriors would want to say to Setanta after he defeated and humiliated them on the field in front of their lord and master?

Write down your ideas in the speech bubbles. Refer back to the text in Chapter Two if necessary.

White Wolves Teachers' Resource
for Guided Reading Year 4
Stories From Different Cultures
© A & C Black 2007

The Hound of Ulster: Teaching Sequence 3

Summary of Chapter Three

The king roars "HALT!" and everyone stops. He is impressed by Setanta and considers allowing him to join his warriors, on condition that he agrees to being looked after by the other boys. Setanta is unhappy about this and turns down an invitation to accompany the king to the blacksmith's feast. He tells him he will join him at Culann's house only after he has fought the boys and proved himself worthy to serve the king. When the king arrives at the home of Culann, his host asks if all his party are present as he has a fierce dog to guard his land which, once loose, will let no man pass. The king, with his mind on the banquet, forgets all about Setanta and tells Culann that it is safe to let the dog loose.

Teaching Sequence

Introduction
Talk about the events of the previous chapter. Who do the group think uttered the "great cry" that prevents Setanta from being killed on the field? What do they think will happen next?

Independent reading
Ask the group to read aloud Chapter Three, focusing on reading for meaning.
- Discuss less familiar words and phrases such as *halt* (p. 26), *good humour* (p. 27), *consider* (p. 28), *newcomer* (p. 29), *strength, courage, valiant* (p. 30), *banquet* (p. 32), *party* (p. 33), *savage beast* (p. 34), *hound, ferociously* (p. 35), *musicians, threaten* (p. 36), *alert* (p. 37).

Returning to the text
Develop children's understanding of the story by asking some of these questions either during reading or at the end of the chapter. Encourage them to find the relevant part in the text to support their answers.

1) How does the king react when Setanta tells him he wants to be one of his warriors? (He laughs, but tells Setanta he is brave and may well become a great warrior (pp. 27–28).)
2) What offer does the king make to Setanta? (The king says he will consider letting Setanta join his warriors if he agrees to let the other boys look after him (p. 28).)
3) How does Setanta respond to the king's offer? (He says, "I don't need anyone to look after me!" (p. 28) and proposes instead to fight every one of the boys instead (p. 30).)
4) What does the king think about Setanta's intention to fight? (He is delighted at the boy's fierceness (p. 29) and impressed by his strength and courage (p. 30).)

Talk about the character of King Conor. Find examples of his kind and considerate nature. For example, he is good humoured when Setanta tells him of his ambition to become a warrior (p. 27); he acknowledges the boy's bravery and ability; he is keen to ensure Setanta's safety (p. 29); he sends word of Setanta's whereabouts to his father (p. 32).

Discuss the interesting array of descriptions the author uses to refer to Culann's dog: *fierce watchdog, savage beast, hound, like a wolf, creature*. Can the children find a simile ("like a wolf") and synonyms (fierce / savage, hound / dog, beast / creature) among the descriptions?
Talk about the way the author has built up tension in the story with the potential threat of the "savage beast".

Next steps
Activity Sheet 3: "I Want to Be…" asks children to write a letter of application from Setanta to the king, asking him to consider employing him as a young warrior. Encourage them to draw on the text as to why Setanta is perfect for the role.

I Want to Be...

Imagine you are Setanta. Write a letter to King Conor, applying for the position of royal warrior.

Remember:
- Use formal language.
- Outline your strengths and abilities.
- State why you would be perfect for the role.

Dear King of Ulster, Conor Mac Nessa,

I write to you most humbly, my lord, in the hope that you will consider doing me the honour of employing me as one of your fine warriors.

_____

_____

_____

_____

_____

_____

_____

_____

_____

_____

The Hound of Ulster: Teaching Sequence 4

Summary of Chapter Four

Setanta emerges victorious from fighting the young warriors. He sets off towards Culann's house to join the king at the feast. Finding the gate locked, Setanta climbs over the wall, unaware of what's on the other side. The guard dog lunges towards Setanta who, still holding his hurley and stone, acts instinctively and flings his stone deep into the beast's throat. Then Setanta hits its head against a rock, killing it dead. Inside, the king hears the creature's final roar and remembers inviting Setanta to the feast. He orders his men outside to see if anything can be done to save Setanta's life.

Teaching Sequence

Introduction
Recap briefly on the events of the story so far. Will Setanta survive the fighting? What will his next challenge be?

Independent reading
Ask the group to read aloud Chapter Four, focusing on reading for meaning.
- Discuss less familiar words and phrases such as *mercy* (p. 38), *whacking* (p. 39), *stomach* (p. 40), *stride* (p. 41), *enclosure* (p. 42), *bared its teeth* (p. 43), *alas* (p. 44), *offended, bloodcurdling, homestead* (p. 45), *innocent* (p. 46).

Returning to the text
Develop children's understanding of the story by asking some of these questions either during reading or at the end of the chapter. Encourage them to find the relevant part in the text to support their answers.
1) What was the outcome of the fighting with the young warriors? (Every one of them had ended up begging Setanta for mercy (p. 38).)
2) How did Setanta react when the guard dog let out "the sort of howl that would freeze your

blood just to hear it" (p. 41)? (He was too hungry and excited to be put off. He was keen to join the king and tell him about his victory (p. 41).)
3) What does the dog's "bloodcurdling" final roar remind the king of? (He remembers that he asked Setanta to follow him and he fears that he has led an innocent child into "the jaws of a wolf" (p. 45).)

The author does not describe the scene where Setanta fights and defeats the young warriors, other than to say that every one of them "ended up begging for mercy" (p. 38). What do the group think about this? Is the effect of leaving the fight scene to the reader's imagination more powerful than describing it in every detail?

Discuss how, once again, Setanta finds himself an unwelcome intruder in a hostile setting. On the field, he had had to defend himself against the king's young warriors. Now he faces an even greater threat: an angry, savage beast.

Talk about the description of the guard dog letting out "the sort of howl that would freeze your blood". What is the effect of this image? Compare this with the description later in the chapter: "a chill ran through the king's heart" (p. 44).

The children could "hot-seat" the king, asking him questions about his actions and emotions. Does he feel remorse about leading an innocent boy into a potentially fatal situation?

Next steps
The children can now complete Activity Sheet 4: "The Defeat of the Savage Beast", which asks them to write about the destruction of Culann's ferocious beast using descriptive words and phrases from the book.

The Defeat of the Savage Beast

Write about Setanta's brave destruction of Culann's savage beast. Use words and phrases from the story to describe the terrifying creature.

_____

_____

_____

_____

_____

_____

_____

_____

_____

_____

_____

_____

_____

_____

_____

savage beast

sound

**bared
its teeth**

creature

**jaws
of a wolf**

hound

White Wolves Teachers' Resource
for Guided Reading Year 4
Stories From Different Cultures
© A & C Black 2007

The Hound of Ulster: Teaching Sequence 5

Summary of Chapter Five

The Ulstermen rush outside and find Setanta standing over the dead hound. The guard carries Setanta inside, where the king expects to hear the worst. Setanta is cheered as he recounts how he killed the ferocious animal, and the king hugs and praises him. But Culann is not happy. He weeps at the loss of his beloved dog and worries that, without it he cannot keep his family safe. Setanta offers to guard his house and land until he can find another. The king approves of this plan and promises to find and train another dog for Culann. Setanta is named Cuchulainn, the Hound of Culann as a mark of his courage and strength.

Teaching Sequence

Introduction
Talk about the challenges that Setanta has overcome in the story so far. Will the king reward him for the strength and courage he has shown?

Independent reading
Ask the group to read aloud Chapter Five, focusing on reading for meaning.
- Discuss less familiar words and phrases such as *weapons, enclosure* (p. 47), *guard* (p. 48), *assembled company* (p. 50), *lamented* (p. 51), *grimly* (p. 52), *serve, replace* (p. 54), *protector' scour the land, breed, reared* (p. 55).
- Help with the pronunciation of the name *Cuchulainn, the Hound of Culann.*

Returning to the text
Develop children's understanding of the story by asking some of these questions either during reading or at the end of the chapter. Encourage them to find the relevant part in the text to support their answers.
1) How do people react to the news that Setanta is safe? (They are astonished and delighted; they cheer the boy for his courage (p. 50). The king hugs and praises Setanta. But Culann is unhappy; he has lost a good friend and his family are no longer safe (pp. 51–52).)
2) What does Setanta propose? (He offers to guard Culann's house and lands until another guard dog is found (p. 54).)

Discuss the significance of Setanta's new name, Cuchulainn, given to him as a mark of his courage and strength. Recall how for much of the story, Setanta's name has not been used. Talk about the pride that he would take from his new name. Whereas once he had little identity, now he is famous as he always dreamed he would be.

Talk about the king's prophetic words: "You will grow to be a great warrior and, in time, the men of Ireland and Scotland shall hear tell of your deeds and fear shall run through their bones" (p. 56). Discuss how the story has been handed down from one generation to the next and has become part of the Celtic story tradition. Why has the story stood the test of time? What relevance does it have for modern readers?

What would Setanta's parents think if they knew of their son's great achievements? The group could explore this idea through role play, with one child interviewing Setanta's parents about their famous son, and the way in which he has risen from poverty to become the celebrated leader of the Red Branch Knights. Would they feel proud? Might they have preferred him to choose a less dangerous role in life, such as a shepherd like his father?

Next steps
The children can now complete Activity Sheet 5: "What's on the King's Mind?", which asks them to write about what King Conor Mac Nessa is thinking at different points in the story.

What's on the King's Mind?

Write about what the king is thinking at different points in the story. Refer back to the text if necessary.

King surveys hurley field	King invites Setanta to join him
_____	_____
_____	_____
_____	_____
_____	_____
King hears the hound roar	**King finds out Setanta is alive**
_____	_____
_____	_____
_____	_____
_____	_____

White Wolves Teachers' Resource
for Guided Reading Year 4
Stories From Different Cultures
© A & C Black 2007

Record Card

Group: **Book:**

Focus for Session:

Names	Comments

Record Card

The White Wolves Interview:
James Riordan

James Riordan has written over 100 books for young people. His first novel, *Sweet Clarinet*, won the NASEN award and was shortlisted for the Whitbread Prize, and *Match of Death* won the Scottish Book Award. In his spare time, he is Visiting Professor at Worcester University.

He lives in Portsmouth, where he may be seen cycling along the seafront with his cat Tilly in a basket.

If you were to appear in the puppet master's show, which character would you be and why?
Petroushka, because I am neither strong nor handsome, a follower not a leader; I act stupid and adore applause. I live in my own little box of a flat, with my cat Tilly for company.

How does retelling a folk tale in a new way compare with writing a story from scratch?
With a folk tale, you already have a framework, the bare bones; you have the setting (forest, snow, wooden hut) and the characters. You must remain true to the original folk tale, but you must make it interesting for today's young readers from a different culture.

Describe the place where you like to write.
I sit at a bit oak table by a window overlooking the sea (if I crane my neck). I have to be absolutely alone (I even kick the cat outside) so that I can feel myself part of the story.

What sort of stories do you enjoy reading?
I read little; except that I read and reread the stories that I write. When I read, it is almost always non fiction, for example at the moment, I am reading a book on the 50 greatest marathons of all time (bit pathetic, eh?).

The White Wolves Interview:
Andrew Fusek Peters

Andrew Fusek Peters is a prolific author for young people with over 60 titles written, many with his wife Polly. Andrew also performs in schools, bringing his books to life with didgeridoo and some mean juggling.

Andrew is the tallest writer in the UK – six foot, eight inches! Find out about his books on www.tallpoet.com.

He lives in a converted chapel in Shropshire, with two children and a goldfish.

Why do you think it is that the story of Anansi appeals to readers of every age and culture?

I always think that trickster tales have an appeal – Anansi has been set an impossible task but that doesn't stop her – her ingenuity, the way she comes up with ideas to outwit the sky god is wonderful. It's also a great metaphor for how stories came to spread among the people

– a story about stories!

What sort of stories do you enjoy reading?

Of course I love all sorts of tales with a twist, ghost stories, and for longer stories – thrillers filled with cliffhangers, where the baddies get done in at the end.

How does retelling a folk tale in a new way compare with writing a story from scratch?

You are always looking for a fresh way to bring a story to life – for me this lies in humour and wordplay – Shakespeare took the bones of old folk tales as the basis for many of his plays and took them in an entirely fresh direction.

Describe the place where you like to write.

I live with my wife and children in a converted chapel in the Shropshire countryside. My office is in the attic, and I look out over our village, the local church and to the hills behind. I am a very lucky writer!

The White Wolves Interview:
Malachy Doyle

Malachy Doyle grew up in a little town near Belfast. After spells as a Polo Mint packer, an advertising executive and a Special Needs teacher, he now writes full time.

Malachy has written more than 60 books, from pop-ups to teenage novels. He has a great fondness for folk tales, and the story of Cuchulainn has always been one of his favourites.

You can find out more about Malachy and his books on www.malachydoyle.co.uk.

Why do you think it is that *The Hound of Ulster* appeals as much to modern readers as to previous generations?

It's a lively, sporty story of a brave young boy winning out against all the odds. It says dreams are achievable, as long as you never stop believing in yourself. It's just a great story – the sort that people have always loved, and always will.

How does retelling a folk tale in a new way compare with writing a story from scratch?

Folk tales have survived down the centuries because they still have something important and entertaining to say. When retelling them, it's essential to keep faith with the truth and the heart of the story, while making them work for the readers of today. Writing a story from scratch is in some ways easier, because you don't have the weight of myth and history leaning on your shoulder, but in some ways harder, because they come from nowhere but your own imagination. I love doing both!

What sort of stories do you enjoy reading?

I've always loved folk tales, but I also read lots of picture books, teenage novels and adult fiction. I love stories that make me laugh or cry – some of the best ones can even do both. I need to believe in the characters, and care passionately about their fate.

Describe the place where you like to write.

My favourite place to work is at my desk, in my great big writing room. It has a wonderful view out over the Irish Sea, which I can rest my eyes on while I sink into the world of story.

White Wolves Resources for Guided Reading

Year 3

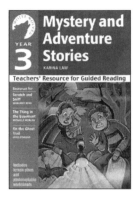

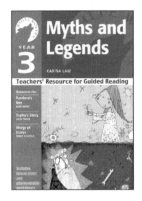

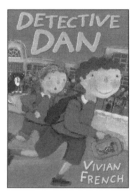

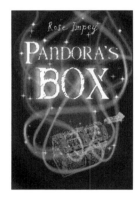

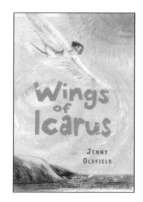

White Wolves Resources for Guided Reading

Year 4

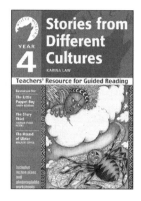

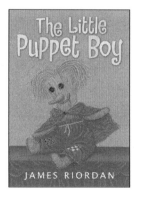

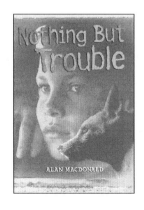

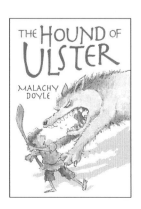

White Wolves Resources for Guided Reading

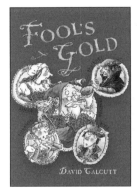

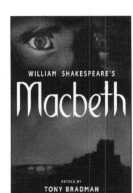

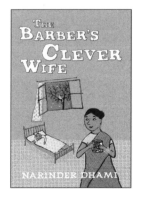

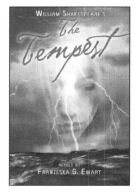